KT-417-967

Contents

Back to school

Today I went back to school.

60 000 105 816

My New Class

WAYLAND

Northamptonshire Libraries
& Information Service

60 000 105 816

Peters	20-Dec-2010
C372.12	£5.99

First published in 2010
by Wayland

Text copyright © Claire Llewellyn
Photograph copyright © Wayland,
except the background of p22 © Istock
and the graphic on p18 © Istock

Wayland
338 Euston Road
London NW1 3BH

Wayland Australia
Level 17/207 Kent Street
Sydney, NSW 2000

The rights of Claire Llewellyn to be
identified as the Author of this Work
have been asserted by her in accordance
with the Copyright, Designs and
Patents Act, 1988.

All rights reserved

Series Editor: Louise John
Editor: Katie Powell
Design: D.R.ink
Photographer: Andy Crawford
Consultant: Shirley Bickler

A CIP catalogue record for this book is available
from the British Library.

ISBN 9780750263764

Printed in China

Wayland is a division of Hachette Children's
Books, an Hachette UK Company
www.hachette.co.uk

With thanks to the children and staff
of Chilton Primary School.

Every effort has been made to clear copyright.
Should there be any inadvertent omission,
please apply to the publisher for rectification.

I am in a new class. I am in Year 1.

My new classroom

This is my new classroom.

It is big and it has
lots of books in it.

My new teacher

I have a new teacher.
Her name is Mrs Foster.

I told her that we went
to the beach on holiday.

Writing a story

Mrs Foster told us to write a story about our holiday.

This is my story and
my picture of us in the sea.

Playtime

At playtime we all ate
a snack. I had a pear.

Then we went in the big playground and played on the slide.

Numbers and counting

After playtime we did some counting.
Mrs Foster put some numbers on the board.

5   12   3
20   18
0   15   7

"Can you show me
the biggest number?"
she said.

School dinner

This year we have school dinner in the big hall.

Chicken and vegetables

Melon

I sat next to Mark and Jenny.
We had chicken and vegetables
and melon.

Running and jumping

In the afternoon we did P.E. We put on our P.E kit and played a running and jumping game.

Then we played a throwing game.

Home time

Then it was time to go home.
Mum was in the playground.
She said, "Hello, big boy!"

Yes, I am big now.
I am in Year 1.

Tell the story

These photos will help you tell the story of my new class. Can you put them in the right order?

START READING is a series of highly enjoyable books for beginner readers. **The books have been carefully graded to match the Book Bands widely used in schools.** This enables readers to be sure they choose books that match their own reading ability.

Look out for the Band colour on the book in our Start Reading logo.

The Bands are:

Pink Band 1A & 1B

Red Band 2

Yellow Band 3

Blue Band 4

Green Band 5

Orange Band 6

Turquoise Band 7

Purple Band 8

Gold Band 9

START READING books can be read independently or shared with an adult. They promote the enjoyment of reading through satisfying stories and non-fiction narratives, which are supported by fun illustrations and photographs.

Claire Llewellyn has written many books for children. Some of them are about real things like animals and the Moon, others are storybooks. Claire has two children, but they are getting too big for her books now. She hopes you will enjoy reading them instead!